Tall Tales

Tall Tales of BisonBear & SchnauzerWorm and
Tall Tales of Bearded Sage & Bantering Battle.

Dorothea Langevin

BALBOA
PRESS
A DIVISION OF HAY HOUSE

Balboa Press books may be ordered through booksellers or by contacting:

Balboa Press
A Division of Hay House
1663 Liberty Drive
Bloomington, IN 47403
www.balboapress.com
1 (877) 407-4847

Print information available on the last page.

ISBN: 978-1-9822-2416-5 (sc)
ISBN: 978-1-9822-2418-9 (hc)
ISBN: 978-1-9822-2417-2 (e)

Library of Congress Control Number: 2019903431

Balboa Press rev. date: 03/23/2019

Tall Tales

Of Bearded Sage

& Bantering Battle

...where trees aren't merely trees!

20 Interactive Enchanted Woodland Tales
for the Inner Child

Photo-Poetry-Prose
by
Dorothea Langevin

"Tall Tales of Bearded Sage & Bantering Battle"
by Dorothea Langevin

Contents

What's Real?

Pathways under bark – unseen,
until the cover's stripped off clean,
a secret message carved in skillful sculptor,
leaves a riddle for our logic-minded culture:

What's illusion, what is real, can we trust our eyes?
to see what clearly cannot be ... and therefore must be lies?
Since, rationale based on the known,
expects to see what would be prone.

Yet, some truths are hidden in plain-view's disguise
seen only by a heart, that's open to surprise.

"Tall Tales"
– Dorothea Langevin 12/2017

Bantering Battle

Woodlands are the place, they say,
where magic creatures roam and soar,

where fiercely fighting forest foes
engage in battle's roar.

But not to worry, that one might
suffer from deadly harm,
for all you see is in the end
just an enchanted charm.

"Tall Tales of Bearded Sage and Bantering Battle"
- Dorothea Langevin 12/2017

Castle Guard

Woodland Gates
to magic realms,
    forest castles
    guarded well,
calling you into their spell.

When you enter,
    magic happens,
    everywhere you turn;
guardians will guide the way,
follow them without delay.

For when you choose
    to be admitted
to the wonder of enchantment,
you will find yourself permitted,
to immigrate a deep entrancement.

Children know this
    without teaching,
that the wonder of the woods,
offers us delightful reaching
into magic's neighborhoods.

"Tall Tales of Bearded Sage and Bantering Battle"
    – Dorothea Langevin 12/2017

Dragon

It's said that dragons
long ago
lived freely all around.

They roamed the woods
on wings so soft
they hardly made a sound.

'Protectors of the Woodland',
that's what they once
were called.

Sadly, disbelief of their fine magic
has kept them grounded here
and stalled.

If you wish to see them fly
on velvet wings once more,

all it takes is to believe
- that they are real -
right within your core.

"Tall Tales of Bearded Sage and Bantering Battle"
- Dorothea Langevin 12/2017

7

Enchanted Castle

Turret, tower, and tall steeple
proudly grace this mighty fort.
Yet, how quiet are its people,
what a hushed royal court?

Seen upon closer inspection
all lively lives asleep
by a spell for their protection
cast by wizards from the keep.

At that time there was a siege
by an evil overlord
who left years ago disgruntled
– all alone he felt quite bored.

Oh, don't worry 'bout them slumber
they will wake again refreshed
in their full and healthy number
feeling safe and so well blessed.

"Tall Tales of Bearded Sage and Bantering Battle"
- Dorothea Langevin 1/20019

Faithful Hunter

A faithful hunter
waiting there
for when his Master shall return,

and claim the prize
which only such
a trusted nose is able to discern.

He's waited for a long time now
but don't you worry not,
a faithful hunter such as he
will hold on to his spot.

"Tall Tales of Bearded Sage and Bantering Battle"
- Dorothea Langevin 12/2017

Of Dwarves

Tales of them fill many books,
for every fairy story
speaks of their unusual looks
and vastly hidden quarry.

Shy of daylight, as is their sort,
so they are seldom seen
outside their deeply caverned fort
sprawled on a log so clean.

This one is resting now
with nightly chores completed,
eyes closed under a heavy brow
into slumber he's retreated.

We'll leave him to it, undisturbed,
retreating quietly and slow
for they are better not perturbed,
since angered they'll put on a show.

"Tall Tales of Bearded Sage and Bantering Battle"
– Dorothea Langevin 12/2018

Lizard Skull

Once, he roamed and slithered
across this wooden land
his favorite spot to doze in
was in the clearing's sand.

He rests there now in stealthy wait
for unsuspecting prey
to come into his sunny glade
right where his head would lay.

As soon as they might settle
perched on a rock near by
he'd start them off their resting spot
and eye them without shy.

"Tall Tales of Bearded Sage and Bantering Battle"
- Dorothea Langevin 1/2019

Last Gladiator

Here comes he now,
the last man standing
in combat battle he gave vow
to bout in fierceness quite outstanding.

The spell, that had him so enslaved
to bid as he was told
a wizard cunningly engraved
on him - a power very old.

Now freedom, that so long he's sought
is there within his roam,
the calling of his lover's love
is guiding him back home.

"Tall Tales of Bearded Sage and Bantering Battle"
- Dorothea Langevin 12/2018

Jester

Every self-respecting royal court
so long ago employed the sort
of witty entertainer who'd delight
his audience with shrewdly phrased insight.

Jesters, then did jokily comment
on life's drama – most lament
about in greatest depth and length;
his witty humor was his greatest strength.

Today, I found his mask just laying there
among the leaves – and heard him laugh, I swear!

"Tall Tales of Bearded Sage and Bantering Battle"
- Dorothea Langevin 12/2018

GriffinLion

A mane-ly head and beak-ed spout,
a GriffinLion - beyond a doubt.

Not to worry, they are mild
mannered fellows in the wild.

So, if you spot one on a tree,
just wave 'Hello' and let him be.

"Tall Tales of Bearded Sage and Bantering Battle"
- Dorothea Langevin - 12/2017

Forest Patrol

If you ever feel
alone, completely unprotected,
know this – with all assurance now –
you never are neglected;

for there's your escort always near
to keep you safe from harm,
the Forest Patrol does guard these woods,
completely undetected.

They watch the sky,
they watch the ground,
they blend in their surroundings;

camouflaged as sticks and leaves,
fooling even seasoned thieves,
they're foiling lurking houndings.

"Tall Tales of Bearded Sage and Bantering Battle"
– Dorothea Langevin 12/2017

Fallen Knight

Right along the forest path
deep in the woods lies he:
The Fallen Knight in armor,
not merely just a tree.
Battle-worn from jousting
with Dragons roaming free.

What once was shiny armor
's now covered deep in moss
all bedded there in comfort.
Who's mourning for his loss?

"Tall Tales of Bearded Sage and Bantering Battle"
- Dorothea Langevin 12/2017

Portal

Many, as they pass this stump
never notice at its base
hidden in this wooden clump
a portal's overgrown encase.

Never used and long forgotten
for its builders are long gone,
timber hinges almost rotten
it's tucked away behind the lawn.

Yet, one fine day, there will come
someone who will recognize
the passage past the entrance's glum,
the treasure hall in wood's disguise.

For, a brave one, who is wise
opens it before he dies
for he knows right from the start
it will lead him to his heart.

"Tall Tales of Bearded Sage and Bantering Battle"
    - Dorothea Langevin 1/19

Swampdragon

Dragons, so they say,
fly high and breeze of fire,
yet, lesser known, a fact it is,
they've cousins in the mire.

There, roaming through the marshy swamps
they slither through the water,
and revel in their muddy romps,
while hunting for their fodder.

Their wings encrusted with debris
from wetland's vegetation
they seldom fly now - though, once, with glee
they soared above the nation.

"Tall Tales of Bearded Sage and Bantering Battle"
- Dorothea Langevin 7/2018

The Bearded Sage

His face in profile on a stump
when I first saw it, made me jump
so unexpected was this sighting
yet very clear in the right lighting.

He's laughing here about my jolt
because for him this joke is old,
ancient in fact, as so is he
who smirks at me from this cut tree.

A friendly sort with wicket humor
I guess they are not just a rumor.

"Tall Tales of Bearded Sage and Bantering Battle"

The Fortress

Once as barricade it stood
perched up high in ancient wood,
the fortress - blackened now with soot,
then considered proud caput.

Battles - fierce - it did withstand
assaults, a steely band
of palisaded walls well manned,
it's force know in the land.

Ruins now, are what remain
of power's mighty reign,
broken the ancestral chain,
their victory in vein.

"Tall Tales of Bearded Sage and Bantering Battle"
- Dorothea Langevin 1/2019

The Tournament

In days long gone and long ago
before we watched the nightly show
on television or video
to tournaments the folk would go;

where brave young lads engaged in battle
so fiercely testing their own strength
with rivals or with winged cattle
or other foes held at arm's length.

Thrill and excitement filled the air
the audience jumped from their chair,
the tryst was swift, the meeting fast ...
... but such jousting's now long past.

"Tall Tales of Bearded Sage and Bantering Battle"
- Dorothea Langevin 12/2018

The Weald-y-Caller

One of these creatures can be heard
from many miles away
their shrieked wail – trust me on that
can't be mistaken for a bird.

Their siren sound alarms
the forest fowl and game
of any mischievous attack
of any foreign arms.

So, if you ever plan
to enter woods unseen
beware of ears that miss no sound
for hearing all, they can.

"Tall Tales of Bearded Sage & Bantering Battle"
- Dorothea Langevin 1/19

37

Unicorn

Some say, the Unicorn: A product of imagination!
However, how can that explain
the sighting of such marvelous creatures
in view of day so plain.

Here lies one now, found dreaming
of dancing in the moonlit wood
with fellow 'fiction' creatures,
while doubters doubt they should.

"Tall Tales of Bearded Sage and Bantering Battle"
- Dorothea Langevin - 7/2018

woodland wizard

It's easy to assume
him simply an uprooted tree,
fooling those who're unaware
is what he does with glee.

For those who wander through his woods
completely inattentive,
he might decide could benefit
from serving as apprentice.

He knows the spells,
he knows the charms,
he's studied them for eons,
only know that once you're called
you might become his peon.

So be alert when journeying
through woodland he inhabits,
and heed advice to stay away,
that's whispered by the rabbits.

"Tall Tales of Bearded Sage and Bantering Battle"
– Dorothea Langevin 12/2017

My Heart-Felt Thanks are to:

- my friends and family – my gracious test-reading & sound-boarding angels, who allowed me to see this book through the eyes of the reader's inner child.

- my Balboa team for calling me 'out of the blue' to invite me to publish my creative expression. For NOT pressuring me into a deadline for the manuscript, which would have made it die a silent death in some forgotten file organizer, and for making this process so easy and fun.

- my mother for instilling in me the love for reading, the love for language, and the love of brilliant and silly wordplay. She gave us the gift of introducing books as a means of inspiration and comfort.

- my father, who took his family on camping trips throughout Western Europe, opening my eyes, ears, nose, heart, taste buds to new and wondrous experiences in a wide range of cultural settings. Evenings were filled with stories from his youth, his warm bass voice inviting us on time-travel adventures.

- my sisters for believing in me, encouraging me, and more or less gruntingly allowing me to tag along on their childhood adventures through our woodland paradise. I'm forever grateful for shared stories and insight into memories – as only siblings can.

- my guys: my late husband and my two sons – all three kids at heart! Their sense of humor – witty and bright – their playfulness and talent of keen observation. For many hours of reading bedtime stories while snuggling close, and countless shared tales we enjoyed at the local library; and their patience with my outbursts in laughter over my own jokes.

I dedicate this book to them – with all my love.

Dear Reader:

I'd love to hear about your response to this book and what enchanted portal it might have (re-) opened for you.

Dorothea Langevin
P.O.Box 844
Middlebury, VT
05753
U.S.A.

Introduction

How it all started...

When asked where the inspiration for this book came from, I'd have to say it all started during Potty Training.

While perched on the 'throne' in the bathroom of the house I grew up in, I had 'time to kill', and as a child I was eager to find something entertaining while waiting. From the relative heights of my post I had a great overview over the floor tiles, which sported a black and white 'ink spilled on water' type design. Tilting my head this way and that way, I suddenly saw faces in the squiggly contours; some friendly smiles, some comical expressions, and even some rather disgruntled looking grimaces.

All of them were practically begging to have me make up a stories around their particular expressions. Maybe back then I did not rhyme the words, but the tale for each, and their connection to each other, were so easily seen through my child eyes.

Most likely I forgot all about my actual mission that had me deposited in the bathroom in the first place, but I was certainly thoroughly entertained and did not mind the required sittings...

... How to enjoy this book...

Just as I once did with the floor tiles, I encourage you to turn the images this way and that way, maybe even upside down. One never knows what might be found in changing perspective. Don't be dismayed, if what you see is not seen by others; not all secrets are revealed to all in the same way. There is no right or wrong way of exploring this book, however, I encourage a good amount of playfulness and fun to be part of the individual equation, which brings me to...

... Ways of seeing...

Spotting the unusual found a new application when I got my first camera at age 11, and I have found the possibilities of 'catching the moment' exciting ever since. Even more, I have always felt the camera lens to be a magnificent looking glass that revealed a deeper sense of what we call 'reality'. Quite often I felt if I focused my viewer just right I could see beyond the surface of the medium I was taking a picture of, be it faces of people or faces of flowers - or now tree trunks.

As an adult - years after being scolded for 'wasting a whole role of film' on photographing a snowman I had built - I realized I had taken a 24-exposure study of said subject. I still love studies of the same object, since every angle and light reflection offers a new insight, and shows a different detail. Digital photography has brought ease and expanded options available at our finger tips to 'tickle out' a deeper reality behind the obvious. Often, I feel compelled to take pictures of a tree trunk and only later on my computer am seeing the 'face', or the 'creature' I've captured.

And just as decades before, each expression appearing before me offers a story I am thoroughly enjoying to tell...

... Speaking of Telling: My Love for Language ...

English, is not my first language. I was born and raised in Germany. Both my parents had lived in the U.S. and English was spoken at home, mainly when the adults did not want us children to understand what they were discussing. What a great incentive for us kids to learn the language!

So, not only did I learn about the power of words to share (secret) messages, I also inhaled the inherent music of language. On summer camping trips with my family my young ears learned to appreciate the melodics of Italian, French and Spanish, and the enchanting lilt of Northern European languages - quite a contrast to the more staccato rhythm of the formal German. Yet, even in my native tongue there is great variation from region to region. Only recently have I found myself rhyming away in the dialect of my region, which has it's very own melody...

...Speaking of poetry...

It's rather funny that I have found poetry to be my medium; funny because after suffering through 'dissecting poetry' in German Literature Class in High School I was fast determined never to use this style of writing. It was introduced to me as having strict rules, clearly identifiable styles. Certain words and phrases from each era had a clear meaning; there was a sense of either getting a poem right or wrong in it's correct interpretation. The approach felt too 'boxed in' for me to find enjoyment in this style of writing.

However, years later as I found myself translating marketing texts from German into English during my corporate career. There, I started to fully appreciate the beauty of language, the power of expression, and the subtle cultural differences expressed in phrases. Particularly in the language style of marketing, which often required as few words as possible to convey the message. Suddenly, I found myself looking at poetry from a whole new point of view of possibility.

The marketing world taught me to take a certain liberty in writing - for me that was finding 'gold'.

As a result, I now claim in my own writing plenty of 'poetic license' in spelling and punctuation, often letting creative inspiration overrule the left-brain logic. After all, this is inspired writing, rather than planned prose. I've come to understand, that every word - in any language - has a unique frequencial signature, set by it's original intent and colored by the meanings it's morphed into since. I've learned to trust, that the words I am guided to choose (as well as the surrounding and supporting punctuation) are what's meant to be written. Who knows some day, these new word creations I'm inspired with might appear in the dictionary, or a newly discovered animal species encyclopedia...

... of Tall Tales...

One of my all-time favorite rainy-day past-time feel-good activities in my early teens was reading fairytales. I especially remember two whopper volumes of collections of "Märchen" filled with lesser known fantastic stories. Each of them offering a world all of its own in which a young girl could immerse herself beyond any sense of 'real' time and space.

I'd feel with the characters, become one with them, and when the tale ended, I'd ponder the plot and spin alternate versions and endings in my head. When you allow yourself to let go of 'right vs. wrong' ... the possibilities are endless...

Each of the photo-poetry tales in this collection before you now was inspired by what the trees cared to reveal on my woodland walks. Thus, my stories are not planned ahead, or logically plotted out, but rather emerged organically.

My camera would capture the image of a character, and often I'd 'hear' its name or theme, which would become the title of the tale. At home, as I'd work with the photo on the screen to enhance what I had glimpsed, I'd 'hear' the first few words and the melody of the poem. I'd have no clear expectation of where the tale would take me, in fact allowing myself to simply stay curious brought forth the magic of this process.

From my translating years I've come to appreciate on-line tools like: 'thesaurus.com', 'Word Etymology', 'Google Dictionary', 'Webster' & friends, and most recently 'rhymezone.com'. My curious mind would wonder, what word might rhyme with 'knight' or 'trunk'. I'd get excited about the various flavors of synonyms to a word and their often surprising, and not seldom forgotten original meaning. This became my 'archeological dig' into the history of language culture.

Each page contains it's own potential plot for a fantastic tale, only waiting to be spun along...

... and lastly...

Just like the each floor tile had its own story line, each of my photos contains a story within itself that inspired the word-play. I love funny word-bantering, mostly to entertain myself – as my kids can attest (while rolling their eyes smirkingly) whenever I shower them with my latest fun-formulations. Laughter is such a freeing expression of emotion. I hope you choose to laugh often! Simply allow your inner kid to explore, and feel the rhythm of the words.

So, if this book shall possibly entertain you, make you smirk or even giggle – it's done more than I initially envisioned.

Yours truly,
Dorothea

Some Inspirations to Interactive Story-Telling:

Each photo-poem is paired with a blank page to encourage you, the reader, to carry on and spin the tale further. Allow yourself to make this book your very own, don't be shy to use markers, crayons, glue and stickers... whatever tickles your fancy.

If you find yourself hesitating to write into the book, maybe the empty space next to each poem becomes your 'movie screen' where you see your version of Tall Tales playing out...

Whichever way you choose to interact with this book - follow your heart, it always leads the way to your enchanted space.

Just as in old-world story-telling tradition, the tale comes to life as it's being told, shared, re-told, and further embellished...

For example:

• Play with rhyming - most fun when spoken out loud - feel the music

• Spot other details in the photo (like "Where is Waldo?")

• Tell the story of what YOU see

• Create a beginning, middle or end to the initial poem I've written

• Take markers, crayons, stickers, glue (scrapbook style) and unleash your (inner) child

• Let the blank canvas page inspire your inner visions to come to life.

• Share your creation with a loved-one, friend, with me - I love to see how my work inspires others...

Enjoy!

My Heart-Felt Thanks are to:

- my friends and family – my gracious test-reading & sound-boarding angels, who allowed me to see this book through the eyes of the reader's inner child.

- my Balboa team for calling me 'out of the blue' to invite me to publish my creative expression. For NOT pressuring me into a deadline for the manuscript, which would have made it die a silent death in some forgotten file organizer, and for making this process so easy and fun.

- my mother for instilling in me the love for reading, the love for language, and the love of brilliant and silly wordplay. She gave us the gift of introducing books as a means of inspiration and comfort.

- my father, who took his family on camping trips throughout Western Europe, opening my eyes, ears, nose, heart, taste buds to new and wondrous experiences in a wide range of cultural settings. Evenings were filled with stories from his youth, his warm bass voice inviting us on time-travel adventures.

- my sisters for believing in me, encouraging me, and more or less gruntingly allowing me to tag along on their childhood adventures through our woodland paradise. I'm forever grateful for shared stories and insight into memories – as only siblings can.

- my guys: my late husband and my two sons – all three kids at heart! Their sense of humor – witty and bright – their playfulness and talent of keen observation. For many hours of reading bedtime stories while snuggling close, and countless shared tales we enjoyed at the local library; and their patience with my outbursts in laughter over my own jokes.

I dedicate this book to them – with all my love.

Dear Reader:

I'd love to hear about your response to this book and what enchanted portal it might have (re-) opened for you.

Dorothea Langevin
P.O.Box 844
Middlebury, VT
05753
U.S.A.

Word of Mouth

Two woodland creatures
passing woodland secrets
only woodland creatures
could have known.

To those who listen closely
the whispers can be heard
among the leaves
and branches thrown.

Yet, all to often, we just hear
leaves rusting in the wind,
when all-the-while the forest shares
old secrets in a murmured tone.

"Tall Tales of BisonBear & SchnauzerWorm"
– Dorothea Langevin 12/2017

Whistling Tree

A happy tune
rings through the woods
enchanting and carefree,

if you had ever heard a one
you'd know it as
a Whistling Tree.

They fill the stillness
of the forest
with haunting melodies,

and when the mood strikes
show themselves
to one who's heart still sees.

"Tall Tales of BisonBear & SchnauzerWorm"
– Dorothea Langevin 12/2017

Twin-Snouted Two-Horn

A tall and handsome creature,
he stands in high regard,
for he's sought out as preacher
in all his woodland yard.

His heights is nearly double
that of a land giraffe,
yet highness is no trouble
his balance is so staff.

He spreads insightful knowledge,
freely from elevated perch
- after all, he went to college
in woodland's own high church.

When asked for his opinion
on matters of import,
to quench his questing minion
he offers wise retort:

"The answer, dear, to burning questions
is never found in haste,
for wisdom grows through living
at an observant pace."

"Tall Tales of BisonBear & SchnauzerWorm"
– Dorothea Langevin 1/2019

TurkeSaurus

Carved into lumber clear by hungry sculptor's bite,
the outline of a Saurus reflected in the light.

A turkey-dinosaurus as if he's in the flesh
worked deeply into timber, the markings seem quite fresh.

This prehistoric game, I'm told, was really truly monstrous
its size and wingspan, so it seems, was just beyond preposterous.

However, no need to despair, he was a friendly fowl,
assuring me - a friend of his: the Ornimegalonyx Owl.

"Tall Tales of BisonBear & SchnauzerWorm"
- Dorothea Langevin 1/2019

The Whale

Have you ever once encountered whales in seas of leaves
passing you unhurriedly with much grace and ease;
a sight so surely unexpected,
I'd say, would leave you quite affected.

After all, we know from years of schooling,
that far away from oceans' pooling,
the picture of a swimming whale would be a thorough fooling.

"Tall Tales of BisonBear & SchnauzerWorm"
– Dorothea Langevin – 7/2018

The Weeping Tree

Some say, that trees
don't feel a thing
inanimate they're standing,
and all the common man will see
them quietly expanding
in years of growth till harvest
- with only stumps left standing.

We need their wood
we need their fuel
they serve a purpose after all.
Yet, if we stopped to see we could
consider them without the cruel,
cold calculation of their tall.

Then, we could see them there
with open eyes awaiting
us to acknowledge their true splendor:
For, oh' so willingly they share
their gifts to us in fating
and offer their surrender.

"Tall Tales of BisonBear & SchnauzerWorm"
- Dorothea Langevin 12/2018

63

The StingrayVulture

Neither fish, neither bird
this creature is amazing,
when spotted with a face all furred
into the land he's gazing.

He mostly lives in solitude
now, there a few remaining
where once there was a largely brood
– but he is not complaining.

Quite liking now his quiet wood,
where he roams here and there,
a peaceful mate, however could
him ponder playing pair.

"Tall Tales of BisonBear & SchnauzerWorm"
- Dorothea Langevin 1/2019

The Greeter

Upon the entry in the wood
you hear a soundly bellow,
so clear and loud that no one could
ignore the wordy fellow.

He is the Greeter here, you know,
has done the job for ages,
he knows you're coming – for the crow
above him so rampages.

To welcome those, who wander here
has been a custom in this park
for there are rules one must adhere
– they're written in the bark.

The woodsy laws are simple, so
there's no need to dismay,
for those you heed them as they go,
enjoy a peaceful rich display.

However, them, who come and thrash
heart-thoughtless through the green
the twigs remind with stinging lash:
"Of cordial conduct we are keen."

"Tall Tales of BisonBear & SchnauzerWorm"
– Dorothea Langevin 2/2019

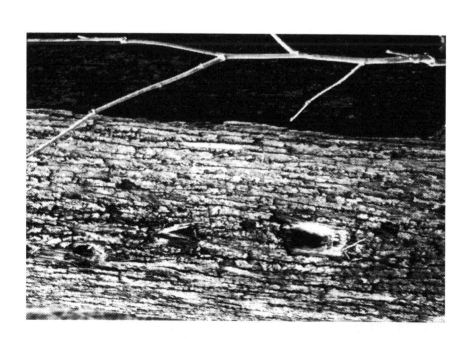

Snout in a Tree

A snout
protruding from a tree
to sniff the morning air,

stirred
out of winter's slumber,
I hope without a care.

A creature
of enchanted woods
reminds me once again,

that forests are the
wonderlands
where childhood dreams began.

"Tall Tales of BisonBear & SchnauzerWorm"
- Dorothea Langevin 12/2017

Sleeping Shepherd

There, along the riverbed,
just by the grassy meadow,
a sheep herd with a many head
was grazing in the summer's glow.

The day was long, the day was hot
so it is not surprising,
that the shepherd leaning there
starts dreaming of his cot.

It's been a while, a century,
since he fell fast asleep,
yet have no worries, luckily,
his boarhound tends the sheep.

"Tall Tales of BisonBear & SchnauzerWorm"
– Dorothea Langevin 7/2018

Singing Tree

This chap
stood by the road today,
along my path
he sang.

He sang with soul,
he sang with heart
not caring
if I can

hear what he's singing of
with focus and revere.

A singing tree,
who would have thought,
and sounding so sincere.

"Tall Tales of BisonBear & SchmauzerWorm"
- Dorothea Langevin 12/2017

73

SchnauzerWorm

Laying there
with brizzly features,
hooded eyes,
and slender trunk,
SchnauzerWorms
are quite a sighting;
among the worms
they are the hunk.

Ten feet long
they're said to grow,
in their lifetime
sure and slow.

So, when in future you seek rest
reclining on a fallen log,
the SchnauzerWorm – I can attest,
serves better than a soggy bog.

"Tall Tales of BisonBear & SchnauzerWorm"
– Dorothea Langevin 7/2018

Kissing Trees

Who says trees just co-exist
life-less, disconnected, and unfeeling?

I saw them kissing, and it touched my heart
to see them boldly stealing,

a sweet embrace of lips of bark,
so sizzling, that I felt the spark.

No doubt there are emotions in a tree,
it surely looked like love to me.

"Tall Tales of BisonBear & SchnauzerWorm"
- Dorothea Langevin 12/2017

HogSnake

Sunning itself by the river
lies a HogSnake undisturbed
lashes closed – yet, still I shiver,
fears arise that I will curb.

I was told they're really harmless
from rosy snout down to their tail,
after all what can an armless
creature do who's just a snail.

Now – let's not irritate its senses
with my presence here too much
after all it has defenses
it will use without a grudge.

"Tall Tales of BisonBear & SchnauzerWorm"
- Dorothea Langevin 1/2019

FuzzyFido

Peaking out behind a trunk
FuzzyFido's playful
temperament is quite well known,
and their joyful spunk.

This one here is sure all ears,
patiently alert
in wait of someone who might pass,
he's waited here for years.

He does not mind to lay there still
moss-covered is he now,
yet in his trusted heart he knows
that some day some one will.

"Tall Tales of BisonBear & SchnauzerWorm"
- Dorothea Langevin 1/2019

81

Fellow Traveler

Just on my walk today
on local forest trails
a fellow traveler joined my way,
delighting me with tales.

He's roamed these roads
many a year
constructing odes
with quiet cheer.

We shared our love for poetry,
the language of the ages,
and even though he's 'just a tree'
and tree trunk rings his pages.

So when, one day,
this tree might fall
exposing lyrics as they lay
in tightly layered scrawl.

"Tall Tales of BisonBear & SchnauzerWorm"
– Dorothea Langevin 12/2018

Enchanted Conversation

In an enchanted forest
it's unsurprising - really,
to find OtterSeals and PenguinGeese
conversing rather freely.

So, in my passing, see,
I take pause and marvel at the sight
that two species - so unharassingly -
can talk without a fight.

"Good Day, you two, and compliments
on your model civil interaction,
we humans still have much to learn,
in the art of kind transaction."

"Tall Tales of BisonBear & SchnauzerWorm"
– Dorothea Langevin 7/2018

BoarTree

The BoarTree
is a curious creature.
This one seemed
a tad grumpy
for being woken
by my passing;
however
he granted me
brief audience
in passing.

He has much wisdom
to share
for he is ancient
and has seen all things
often missed.

Just come back
when he is rested
and ready for a chat.

"Tall Tales of BisonBear & SchnauzerWorm"
– Dorothea Langevin 12/2017

BisonBear

The Bison-Bear
  is native to
  the ample woodland regions;
  it roams in forests
    near and far
  and once patrolled in legions.

  In our days
  they are quite rare
  a sight in leafy thickets,
  where free they trek
    forevermore
  not bound by any pickets.

Majestic are these creatures
  truly an enormous sight,
  the wise explorer of the woods
  knows not to pick a fight.

So simply marvel in their massive
  presence when they're spotted,
  and clear a path with all respect –
  they mislike being distraughted.

"Tall Tales of BisonBear & SchnauzerWorm"
– Dorothea Langevin 12/2017

A CougarWolf's Taming

The way to tame a CougarWolf
is with a gentle hand
so to avoid that he'd engulf
his handler from the land.

The trick is simply, I will tell,
to offer him his gourmet treat
he can't resist the tasty smell
of maple leaves – so sweet.

So, if you ever meet a Northern LionHound
I'd recommend you gather quick those leaflets off the ground.

"Tall Tales of BisonBear & SchnauzerWorm"
– Dorothea Langevin 12/2018

What's Real?

Pathways under bark – unseen,
until the cover's stripped off clean,
a secret message carved in skillful sculptor,
leaves a riddle for our logic-minded culture:

What's illusion, what is real, can we trust our eyes?
to see what clearly cannot be ... and therefore must be lies?
Since, rationale based on the known,
expects to see what would be prone.

Yet, some truths are hidden in plain-view's disguise
seen only by a heart, that's open to surprise.

"Tall Tales"
- Dorothea Langevin 12/2017

Contents

Tall Tales

Of BisonBear

& SchnauzerWorm

...where trees aren't merely trees!

20 Interactive Enchanted Woodland Tales
for the Inner Child

Photo-Poetry-Prose
by
Dorothea Langevin

Printed in the United States
By Bookmasters